Can I Tell You About

Dyscalculia?

A Guide for Friends, Family and Professionals

Judy Hornigold

Illustrated by Joe Salerno

Jessica Kingsley Publishers
London and Philadelphia

First published in 2020
by Jessica Kingsley Publishers
73 Collier Street
London N1 9BE, UK
and
400 Market Street, Suite 400
Philadelphia, PA 19106, USA

www.jkp.com

Library of Congress Cataloging in Publication Data
A CIP catalog record for this book is available from the Library of Congress

British Library Cataloguing in Publication Data
A CIP catalogue record for this book is available from the British Library

ISBN 978 1 78775 045 6
eISBN 978 1 78775 046 3

Printed and bound in Great Britain

The Candle

The wooden dragon comes to light my wick
And the little flame grows ever so quick.
My golden hot flame is dancing and waving,
And swiftly and softly it starts swaying.
Little children watch me
As I see my flame reflect in their eyes!
I feel quite sad when there is a friend or foe.
Because it only means I will die out with one
    gentle blow,
And out comes smoke shapes of Arabian
    prancers,
Also great smoke horses which are great
    dancers.

By Kirstie, an 11-year-old dyscalculic girl. Her ambition is to be a playwright. Her assessment showed that in Mathematics, 95 per cent of people are better than her.

Acknowledgements

I would like to thank Aidan Milner for his help in writing this book; his recollections of his childhood have been invaluable. He is an absolute inspiration to anyone with dyscalculia.

Contents

Introduction for Adults 9

About Dyscalculia 14

Early Years 18

Dyscalculia Testing 21

Family 24

At Home 25

Friends 29

Helping Yourself 31

At School 34

How to Help 37

Success 45

Advice for Adults 47

Information and Support 52

Introduction for Adults

The aim of this book is to provide an introduction to dyscalculia for parents, children, family members and friends. Whilst dyslexia is largely understood in society and often well catered for in schools, dyscalculia is very much the poor relation. Many people are unfamiliar with the term and teachers may have had little, if any, training in how to support children with dyscalculia.

Dyscalculia is a specific learning difficulty with numbers that affects around 5 per cent of the population. It is better thought of as a difficulty in arithmetic, rather than in numeracy as a whole, as there may be no difficulty with topics such as shape or geometry. Put simply, dyscalculic people have no clear understanding of quantity. They find it very hard to visualise the numerical magnitude of a number. When they see the symbol 5, they don't have a picture of five items in their mind. Consequently, they struggle with identifying which of two numbers is the larger. They also lack number sense, which means that they find it hard to comprehend our number system and how numbers relate to each other. They will have difficulty in working mentally with the four number operations, addition, subtraction, multiplication and division and have little understanding of the effect of these operations.

Dyscalculia is present from birth and is a lifelong condition that is unrelated to IQ. It can be remediated with good intervention and support. You can find more details about resources and further reading and useful organisations in the information section at the end of the book.

Although there is much less research surrounding dyscalculia compared to other learning difficulties such as dyslexia, it is legally recognised as a disability. This means that schools have an obligation to identify learners with dyscalculia and to put in place reasonable adjustments to ensure that these children have the same opportunities as every other child in the class. A child may be given extra time in tests or exams, or they may have individual or small group learning support. All staff should be aware of the difficulties that dyscalculic learners experience so that they can adjust their teaching to meet the needs of these children.

Numeracy anxiety

Many children will be anxious about numbers at some stage. They often worry about making mistakes and looking stupid if they can't do it. This anxiety or fear of numbers is not the same as having dyscalculia.

People with dyscalculia have severe anxiety about numeracy and will find it very stressful to do numbers in front of other people or under time pressure. Mental calculations can be traumatic and can take much longer than would be expected. In some cases the fear that a dyscalculic person experiences can be paralysing, leaving them unable to think clearly at all.

Children with dyscalculia often have poor self-esteem and may become isolated. They will often avoid playing dice games or games with complex scoring systems as they can't keep track of the numbers.

Dyscalculic children may have strengths in *creativity*. Many dyscalculic children are creative and this is often due to the imaginative ways that they have had to develop to overcome their issues with numbers. This creativity can also lead to high-level skills in strategic thinking and problem solving. These are skills that are highly valued in the workplace today.

Often, dyscalculic people will have an excellent memory for the printed word and may excel in language learning and poetry.

Perseverance and resilience

Dyscalculic children will have to work harder than their peers, and with the right support and encouragement this can lead to them developing resilience and perseverance. These are great life skills that will serve them well as they progress into adulthood.

Dyscalculia need not be a barrier to achieving your potential. A couple of years ago I had the great pleasure of meeting Aidan Milner in New Zealand. He is severely dyslexic and dyscalculic but had worked hard at overcoming these difficulties and at the time was doing a Master's degree in Geology as well as volunteering for the ambulance service on a Friday night. He is an incredibly accomplished young man and testament to the fact that you can achieve success in life even with a specific learning difference.

Professor Paul Moorcraft, a former BBC war correspondent, was described by Professor Brian Butterworth (a leading researcher into dyscalculia) as the most dyscalculic person he had ever assessed. Paul is a Professor of Journalism and Media, and the author of 25 books.

There are also celebrities with dyscalculia such as Cher and Mary Tyler Moore, Mick Hucknall and Henry Winkler.

About Dyscalculia

"Hi, my name is Sam and I have dyscalculia. Dyscalculia means having difficulty with numbers, so it is a bit like being dyslexic and finding reading difficult. Some people find it hard to pronounce the word 'dyscalculia'; I remember it by rhyming it with 'peculiar'.

Out of a hundred children there will be four or five with dyscalculia, but you can't tell just by looking at someone. Dyscalculia is caused by a difference in the way my brain works and means that I find it very hard to understand numbers and how they work together. I sometimes can't tell if one number is larger than another, and it has taken me ages to learn to tell the time. I don't like playing dice games because I have to count the dots on the face of the dice. I can't see the pattern of the dots and match it with a number. I feel embarrassed if I have to do numbers in front of other people. I am worried that they will laugh at me and think that I am stupid.

When I was little no one really noticed that I had dyscalculia. It was only when I went to school and had to start learning to count and to add numbers together that my mum began to wonder why I was finding it so hard. I found reading much easier and just thought that everyone found numbers hard!

$$9 + 5 = 15$$
$$9 + 5 = 11$$
$$9 + 5 = 95$$

Dyscalculia is something that you are born with and it tends to run in families, so if you have it, your parents or your brothers and sisters may have it too. Sometimes people with dyscalculia also have other learning difficulties such as dyslexia or ADHD. Dyscalculia is not related to how intelligent you are, and many people with dyscalculia do very well in other subjects at school. It is important if you are really struggling with Mathematics (or 'Math', as they call it in the US) and there seems to be no particular reason for this, that you get tested at school to see if you have dyscalculia. I struggle with numeracy at school every day but it helps me to know the reason why I am struggling and that my teachers understand why I am finding it so difficult. They have helped me to find ways to make numbers easier to understand and I really enjoy using resources like cubes and ten frames to help me to see how numbers work together. I know that I will always have dyscalculia but I am determined not to let it stop me from doing what I want to do with my life. I didn't always feel this way; when I was younger

I found life very difficult. Let me tell you about my life and how dyscalculia has affected me."

How many ● are there?

Early Years

"When I was little, I found learning to count very hard. I could just about remember the sequence of numbers 1 to 10, but only if I always started at 1, and it was impossible for me to count backwards. Mum used to try to help me by pretending to be launching a rocket and we would count backwards from 10 for take off, but I always got confused and Mum got frustrated. Looking back, now I can see that numbers had no meaning for me. Learning to count was like learning a nursery rhyme, so no wonder I found it hard to count backwards – have a go at reciting 'Jack and Jill' or 'A-Tisket, A-Tasket' backwards and you will see what I mean.

I find it very hard to understand place value.
Sometimes a 1 is a one and sometimes it is a ten
or a hundred, which makes no sense to me. I will
often write numbers with too many zeros, because
to me 'one hundred and two' is written as 100 with
2 next to it, like this: 1002.

I also didn't like playing games with dice, such
as Snakes and Ladders or Yahtzee. My brother
and sister would roll the dice and quickly work
out their move, but it took me ages to work out
how many places I could move as I had to count
the dots and they would shout at me if I moved
the wrong number of spaces. They thought I was
cheating.

Sometimes Mum and Dad would ask me to
help them to lay the table for dinner. It would
take me so long to put out the right number of
plates, knives and forks. Most of the time I would
get it wrong and I think they thought I was just
being lazy.

Nobody imagined then that I had dyscalculia; we didn't even know it existed."

Dyscalculia Testing

"When I was six, my teacher, Mrs Robin, noticed that my numeracy wasn't as good as the other children in my class and that I was falling way behind everyone else. I just could not understand place value and I could not estimate answers either. If I was adding 19 and 32 I would have no idea that the answer would be nearly 50. So I would just believe whatever answer I came up with, even if it was way out. Mrs Robin was surprised because I was very good at English and was very interested in all the other subjects except Mathematics. She spoke to my mum and dad to ask them if she could do some tests to see if there was a problem. By this time, Mum and Dad were also getting a bit worried so they were happy that my teacher was trying to find out what was wrong.

She found a test for dyscalculia that I did on the computer. I had to match dots to numbers, find the larger number from a pair of numbers and do some calculations. It didn't take too long but it made me feel anxious as I knew that I was making lots of mistakes.

The results of the screener showed that I was likely to have dyscalculia. My parents and I did not know what that was – or even how to say it. Mrs Robin explained that it was a difficulty with numbers and that my brain was wired differently from other children. She explained that it wasn't my fault and that there were lots of other people with dyscalculia too. I felt relieved because now I had a reason for why I was finding numbers so hard, and my teacher was relieved because she could now find ways to help me to learn. Mum decided that it would be good for me to have a more detailed test and the school arranged for a specialist tester to come and assess me. This was a longer test and I had to do lots of numeracy. It was quite hard and I was worried because I was getting so many questions wrong and some I just could not understand at all. I felt very tired that evening when I got home from school. The specialist tester agreed that I had dyscalculia and she wrote a long report explaining what dyscalculia was and how it would affect me. She also suggested lots of ways that my family and the school could help."

Family

"**D**yscalculia can be hereditary, but when Mum and Dad were at school, not many people knew about dyscalculia, so they would not have been diagnosed. Dad told me that he found numbers hard and still gets worried if he has to do them quickly or in his head, and he hates doing any numeracy in front of his workmates as he is worried that he might get it wrong. So we think that maybe he has dyscalculia, too. He and I think of it as our 'super power', something that only we have in our family. We have found out about other people who have this super power too, such as Cher and Henry Winkler. It has really helped to know that I have dyscalculia. I am not so worried anymore. My brother and sister don't tease me so much and try to help me if they can see that I am struggling."

At Home

"**M**um likes numbers and has found ways to make numeracy more fun for me. She used LEGO® pieces to help me understand fractions such as a half and a quarter. We used to sing the times tables to songs that I liked in the charts. Mum used everyday things that were around the house to help me as well. She bundled straws into groups of 10 to help me understand place value.

We play games with a different dice and that has helped me to join in more as I can work out my moves more quickly. In fact, Mum seems to find numbers everywhere we go. We count the lampposts on the way to school, we count up and down the stairs at home, and when we go shopping, she asks me to fetch four apples or three oranges. These sorts of activities help me because I am not in a stressful situation and we can take our time.

Telling the time has always been very hard for me. To me a clock is just a circle with confusing lines and numbers on it. I had to get a special watch with the minute and hour hands labelled and all the numbers marked out on the face, which helped as I could see what was going on and it made more sense.

I also find it hard to tell how long an hour is or how long 10 minutes is – sometimes they seem the same to me. So my family and I play games that help me to have a sense of time. We estimate how long we have been on a journey in the car or how long it will take to walk round the park. My dad bought me a set of sand timers that could measure different lengths of time, from one minute to one hour, and that has helped me to know how long I have spent on my homework or on a computer game.

Numeracy at home is now part of everyday life. I still don't really like numbers but I am not as afraid of them anymore."

Friends

"When I was diagnosed with dyscalculia, I explained to my friends what it was. I don't think they really understood at first, but Mrs Robin explained it as well and now they try to help me, and sometimes their explanations are better than Mrs Robin's! A lot of my friends find numbers hard sometimes, too, and although they are not dyscalculic, we work together to solve problems. I much prefer working with a group of friends in Mathematics than working on my own.

Playing games can still be hard as I don't always understand the scoring system, but my friends keep score so that I can join in.

Some of the people in my class weren't as helpful and they would tease me. They teased me a lot about my watch because it was different and they thought it was babyish. That upset me for a while, but my teacher explained to them why I had it and they soon got bored teasing me about it."

Helping Yourself

" I think the more you understand dyscalculia the easier it is to cope with, and it is important that the people around you understand it too. I tell people that dyscalculia means that I find it hard to do numbers, especially mental numbers, and I can't remember times tables and other number facts very well.

Having dyscalculia isn't easy, but it is much easier if your friends and family know about it and understand how difficult it can be for you. When I first found out that I had dyscalculia I didn't really want to tell anybody and I didn't want to ask anyone for help. Now, I have realised that it is a really good idea to tell other people and to ask for help when I need it.

I have found ways around some of the difficulties that I have. I use reminders on my smartphone and I have a calculator with the numbers written in words. I use pictures and diagrams wherever possible to help me understand numbers, and I have a set of cards with key facts and numeracy words on that I practise every day. I know that I will never be good at numbers, but I work extra hard to try and understand the basics. Mathematics is only one part of the school day and I know that there are other subjects that I really enjoy and am really good at.

I have been lucky because my family help me and my teachers have been very understanding. The school have come up with a plan to help me. It is called an Education Health and Care Plan and this makes sure that everyone knows that I have dyscalculia and that they know how to help me. Not everyone has the same experience and sometimes you may find that no one believes you have a learning difference. They may just think you are being stupid. This can be very upsetting and may make you feel very worried that there is something wrong with you. There is nothing wrong with you. You are not the problem. It is just that your brain works differently, and that can be annoying and frustrating, but it can also lead to you having strengths that other children don't have. Dyscalculic people are often very good at solving problems and they can be very inventive. These are great skills to have when you leave school and are looking for an interesting career.

Never ever feel ashamed or embarrassed about having dyscalculia if people make fun of it or tease you. I think you should feel sorry for them, as they are not mature enough to understand.

Having dyscalculia teaches you that you must work hard, and in life you need to work hard to get what you want. No one can stop you from achieving your dreams. Having dyscalculia, I think, gives you an advantage on most people as you have to develop extra skills early on in life."

At School

"**B**efore I was diagnosed, Mathematics lessons were very hard for me. I didn't understand what was going on and I used to get a horrible feeling in the pit of my stomach before each lesson. I tried to copy what my friends were doing but they didn't like that and sometimes they would move away from me.

After Mrs Robin found out that I was dyscalculic she started to make changes to the work that I was given and the equipment that I could use to help me. I also had lessons on my own with a support teacher, Mrs Mann, and I really liked those because I wasn't worried about looking stupid in front of my friends. Mrs Mann is a lovely teacher and is very patient. She explains things in lots of different ways and usually there is one way that makes sense to me. We play lots of games too, which is fun.

My problems with numbers are worse if I am stressed or tired and if I am 'put on the spot' in class. My teachers understand that now, and have made changes to the lessons and the classroom to help me as much as possible. They make sure that I have lots of equipment to help me 'see' the numbers. I like to use base ten materials, ten frames and two-coloured counters. My friends find these resources helpful, too. Before I was diagnosed I was often given simple worksheets to do and my friends would be doing much more difficult calculations. Sometimes it made me feel like crying as I felt stupid and everyone could see how easy my work was, and that I couldn't even do that.

Now, I don't have that horrible feeling in my stomach anymore, and although I still find it very hard, I know that my teacher and my friends will help me and not make me feel bad."

How to Help

At school

"My teachers at school have found many ways to help me, and my friends say that it helps them too, even though they don't have dyscalculia.

These are the top 10 things that really help me:

1. *Using a variety of concrete materials*

    My favourite materials are base ten materials and ten frames. Base ten materials are good for understanding place value. Ten frames help me to understand how numbers work together, especially number bonds to 10. My school also has Cuisenaire rods and these help me to understand fractions and ratios a bit better.

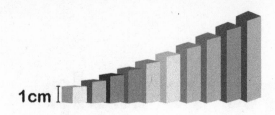

1cm

2. *Not being rushed*

We used to have timed tests in school and I hated them, but now we don't have them and sometimes my teacher gives me fewer questions to do as she knows that it takes me a bit longer.

3. *Learning numbers through games*

My learning support teacher, Mrs Mann, has lots of games to help me with numbers, and one of my favourites is 'shut the box'.

This is a quick game to play and helps me to recognise the value of the dots on a dice and to match it to a number.

4. *Being shown different ways of working things out*

In our Mathematics lessons we explore lots of different ways of solving a problem. Some of my friends understand all of the ways; I usually only understand one or maybe two ways. But it helps me to have lots of different methods so I can choose the one that works for me.

5. *Drawing pictures*

Drawing pictures of the numbers we are doing helps me to imagine it in my head, and when we have tests we can't use the equipment so it helps me to see what is going on if I have a picture of it in my head.

3 x 2 = 6

6. *Learning by doing*

A lot of numeracy seems to be learning rules and facts and this is really hard for me. It is much better if I can be doing something with the equipment to help me find out these rules for myself.

$$7 + 3 = 10$$

7. *Going over things many times*

It can be very frustrating because I think that I have understood something one day and then the next day I have forgotten it. Nothing seems to stick, but it does help if I go over the same thing lots of times. I may need to do it every day for a week or two before it stays in my memory.

8. *Help in understanding the language of numbers*

I am really good at English but words for numbers can be very confusing. I remember thinking that an acute angle must be soft and cuddly, like a kitten.

So now I have a set of cards with the tricky words on and an example or explanation to help me understand.

9. *Not worrying about making mistakes*

My teacher has a display board showing the 'mistake of the week'. This is where she displays the best mistake that someone has made that week. My mistakes are sometimes there and sometimes my friends have made a 'really good' mistake that we all learn from. It really helps me to see where I have gone wrong and I don't feel ashamed about making a mistake.

This was one of my mistakes:

$19 + 13 = 212$

We split this up to help me see where I had gone wrong:

$19 + 13 = 10 + 9 + 10 + 3 = 20 + 9 + 3 =$
$20 + 12 = 20 + 10 + 2 = 30 + 2 = 32$

10. *Having things to help me remember*

Mum made me a little booklet for all the things that I find hard to remember.

It might be a times table fact or the meaning of a numbers word. I take it to school so that I don't have to worry about remembering everything.

Acute Angle   A Cute Angle

At home

We play lots of dice games at home and Dad and I like to play dominoes. I am getting better at recognising the dot patterns on the dice. Sometimes I don't even need to count the dots.

Mum has shown me how to write out a multiplication grid:

X	1	2	3	4	5	6	7	8	9	10
1	1	2	3	4	5	6	7	8	9	10
2	2	4	6	8	10	12	14	16	18	20
3	3	6	9	12	15	18	21	24	27	30
4	4	8	12	16	20	24	28	32	36	40
5	5	10	15	20	25	30	35	40	45	50
6	6	12	18	24	30	36	42	48	54	60
7	7	14	21	28	35	42	49	56	63	70
8	8	16	24	32	40	48	56	64	72	80
9	9	18	27	36	45	54	63	72	81	90
10	10	20	30	40	50	60	70	80	90	100

It took me a long time to begin with but we practised every day and now I can do it in about five minutes. It helps me when I am doing a test at school because I can write it out at the beginning and then I don't need to worry about remembering the tables. I start with an empty 10 x 10 grid and then fill in the ones that are easier for me to do. These are the 1x, 2x, 5x and

10x tables. Dad showed me the pattern in the 9x table so I do that one next. The 4x table is two lots of the 2x table, the 3x table is the 1x and 2x tables added together. By now most of the table has been completed and I can usually work out the others from what I have already filled in."

Success

"There are many famous people with dyscalculia, such as Cher and Henry Winkler, and there is no reason why your dyscalculia should stop you from achieving anything that you want to in your life. You may need to work harder than other people, but that will develop a good way of working for you that will help later in life. Many dyscalculic people have skills that others don't have such as creative problem solving, and many dyscalculics are very good at language.

I want to be an architect when I am older. Jørn Utzon, the designer of the Sydney Opera House, was dyscalculic, and I think that is one of the most impressive buildings in the world.

Remember, having dyscalculia does not mean that you are stupid. I hope that reading this book has helped you to understand a little more about it. Ask your friends, family and teachers to read this book too so that they can understand the problems that you have.

You will have many strengths and skills that will enable you to become whatever you want to be, so don't be afraid to follow your dreams, and don't let dyscalculia get in your way."

Advice for Adults

Dyscalculic children will struggle with:

Understanding numbers: They may not know that 9 is more than 5 because they have not attached a quantity to the number. To them, 9 is a symbol that we call "nine", but it does not conjure up an image of nine items.

Subitising: Subitising is our ability to say how many items there are in a set without actually counting them. Most people, when looking at four biscuits on a plate, would be able to say instantly there were four without counting them. A dyscalculic person does not have this automatic recognition of small quantities and would have to count the biscuits.

Estimation: Dyscalculic children don't have a feel for what the answer may be, so they will accept whatever number they come up with. For example, we know that 34 + 62 is almost 100 but a dyscalculic person may end up with the answer 3462 and not realise that this must be incorrect. On one occasion I placed 15 counters on a table and asked the child I was working with to estimate how many there were. She said 50. Then we counted them to find that there were, in fact, 15. I then added five more counters and asked her to estimate the new quantity. She said eight. This is typical of a dyscalculic person who has not attached a visual image of a numerical quantity to the number name or number symbol.

Counting backwards: Numbers are just words to a dyscalculic person, so counting backwards has no logical structure. They may be able to recite the sequence forwards but have no idea why one number comes after another. Try reciting a familiar nursery rhyme backwards to get a sense of how difficult counting backwards can be for someone with dyscalculia.

Spotting patterns: Being able to spot patterns can make numeracy a whole lot easier, but dyscalculic people find this very hard.

For example:

$$10 + 4 = 14$$
$$20 + 4 = 24$$
$$30 + 4 = 34$$
$$40 + 4 = 44$$

We can see a pattern emerging here, but a dyscalculic child would not see that the next answer will be 54.

Understanding place value: This is a tricky concept for many young children but particularly hard for dyscalculic learners who find it hard to understand that the digit can change value depending on its place in the number. Dyscalculic people will often write 1002 instead of 102 when they hear "one hundred and two", because they have not understood the concept of place value and they write the symbols for the words that they hear.

Time: Learning to tell the time is notoriously difficult, and many children will struggle with this, dyscalculic children particularly so. However, it is not only telling the time that is challenging but also understanding the passage of time. A dyscalculic person may not be able to appreciate whether an hour has passed or only a few minutes.

Children with dyscalculia will need:

- Extra support at school. It may be necessary to have an Education Health and Care Plan (EHCP). An EHCP describes your child's special educational needs and the help that should be provided to meet those needs. This will enable the school to access extra funding to support your child. It may be that the school can provide individually tailored support and classroom accommodations that will meet the needs of your child without the need for an EHCP. You will need to discuss the options with the headteacher and special educational needs coordinator (SENCo) at your child's school.

- Reassurance that their difficulties are not because they are unintelligent; often quite the reverse is true. Dyscalculic children may have had years of experiencing failure in Mathematics before they are diagnosed, and may feel that it is somehow their fault and that they must be stupid.
- Help in developing strategies to cope. There are many computer programs and apps that can help (some of these are detailed at the end of this book).
- To develop self-advocacy skills. Dyscalculic children need to have the courage and willingness to ask for help.

Information and Support

This section details websites, books and resources that you may find helpful. If you feel that you would like your child to have a formal assessment for dyscalculia , you can find an assessor from either PATOSS (www.patoss-dyslexia.org)or the BDA (www.bda-dyslexia.org.uk).

Your child's school may have access to an Educational Psychologist who could also carry out the assessment. The assessor will produce a report detailing recommendations for you as parents and for the school. It may be that individual support is required either 1-1 or in small groups. Sometimes, adjustments to teaching practice would be recommended, for example, using more concrete materials to model the maths and giving the child extra time.

It is important to be aware that your child may be suffering from low self-esteem or maths anxiety and their teachers need to be sensitive to this and to try to rebuild any damaged confidence in Maths. Whilst, naturally, if you are a parent, you will be concerned about your child's attainment in maths, try not to convey your anxieties and keep your support fun and low key. I have detailed some resources below that are fun and non- threatening for children.

Useful websites

The three websites below offer information and advice on dyscalculia. The Dyscalculia Association was set up by the author and Steve Chinn in 2018.

www.dyscalculiaassociation.uk

www.stevechinn.co.uk

www.judyhornigold.co.uk

This is the website of Professor Brian Butterworth and has links to his research, articles and publications. It's an ideal place to go if you already have a basic understanding of what dyscalculia is and how to support dyscalculic children.

www.mathematicalbrain.com

This is the website of the British Dyslexia Association, offering advice, support and training for parents and teachers interested in dyslexia and dyscalculia.

www.bdadyslexia.org.uk

The below four websites offer general advice and information about dyscalculia, including checklists, links to other websites and book recommendations.

www.dyscalculia.org

www.dyscalculia.me.uk

www.aboutdyscalculia.org

www.dyscalculia-Maths-difficulties.org.uk

This is a fun and engaging approach to learning the times tables.

www.muliplicationrules.co.uk

This is an excellent website for games and ideas – aimed at teachers but useful for parents too.

www.ronitbird.com/games

This website has hundreds of maths games and activities aimed at both primary and secondary teachers.

https://nrich.maths.org

Recommended books

By the author

(2014) Dyscalculia Lesson Plans Books 1 and 2.
Nottingham: TTS Group Ltd.
These two books are aimed at teachers planning intervention lessons for children with dyscalculia.

(2015) Dyscalculia Pocketbook.
   Alresford: Teacher's Pocketbooks.
A good explanation of dyscalculia for those
wanting to further their understanding.

(2016) Making Maths Visual and Tactile.
   Wakefield: SEN Books.
Full of ideas for games and activities, aimed at
primary teachers but used by many parents of
dyscalculic children.

(2018) Understanding Maths Learning Difficulties.
   Maidenhead: Open University Press.
This book is aimed at professionals who are
seeking a qualification in dyscalculia and maths
difficulties.

By other authors
The following books are mainly aimed at teachers.
The titles in bold would also be suitable for
parents wishing to find activities and games to
support a dyscalculic child.

Ronit Bird (2013) *Dyscalculia Toolkit: Supporting Learning Difficulties in Maths*. London: Sage Publications Ltd.

Ronit Bird (2011) **The Dyscalculia Resource Book**. London: Sage Publications Ltd.

Brian Butterworth and Dorian Yeo (2004) *Dyscalculia Guidance: Helping Pupils with Specific Learning Difficulties in Maths*. Abingdon: nferNelson

Steve Chinn (2004) **The Trouble with Maths**. London: Routledge Falmer.

Steve Chinn (2012) *More Trouble with Maths*. London: Routledge.

Steve Chinn (2018) *Maths Learning Difficulties, Dyslexia and Dyscalculia*. London: Jessica Kingsley Publications.

Jane Emerson and Patricia Babtie (2013) *The Dyscalculia Assessment*. London: Bloomsbury.

Jane Emerson and Patricia Babtie (2014) **The Dyscalculia Solution**. London: Bloomsbury.

Linda Pound and Trisha Lee (2015) *Teaching Maths Creatively*. London: Routledge.

Other resources

Crossbow Education, a family business started in 1992 by SEN teacher Bob Hext:

www.crossboweducation.com

Steve Chinn Dyscalculia Toolkit
This is a collection of resources to use when teaching/supporting children with dyscalculia (sold on above website).

SEN Books

Judy Hornigold (2016) *Making Maths Visual and Tactile: A Compendium of Games and Activities to Teach Key Number Skills*. Wakefield: SEN Books. This is a box of equipment to complement the book of the same title.

Sarah Wedderburn (2019) *Diagnostic Assessment of Numeracy Skills*. Wakefield: SEN Books. This is a screening kit used for identifying learners with dyscalculia in the classroom.

TTS (www.tts-group.co.uk)

Dyscalculia Lesson Plans Kit

Dyscalculia Games

Dyscalculia Problem Solving Cards

Two-coloured counters

Sand timers

Ten frames

Cuisenaire rods

Base ten materials

Findel (www.findel-international.com)

Kate Ruttle, *Target Ladders, Dyscalculia.*

Addacus (www.addacus.co.uk)

This is a great resource for teaching place value.

Apps

Call Scotland have a wheel of iPad apps for learners with dyscalculia and numeracy difficulties, which can be found at:

www.callscotland.org.uk/common-assets/ cm-files/posters/ipad-apps-for-learners-with- dyscalculianumeracy-difficulties.pdf

IT resources in the UK

Nessy numbers, designed to help students of all abilities learn to read, write, spell and type:

www.nessy.com/uk

Wordshark, provides a fun and effective solution for students learning to read and spell:

www.wordshark.co.uk

Maths Explained videos by Steve Chinn:

www.stevechinn.co.uk

Number Sense games:

www.numbersense.org.uk

The Number Race game:

www.thenumberrace.com

IDL numeracy software overview:

www.idlsgroup.com/numeracy

Dynamo Maths identifies and supports pupils at risk of developmental dyscalculia, and pupils who are performing significantly below their peers:

www.dynamomaths.co.uk

Number Gym, specialist software for school and home:

www.numbergym.co.uk

The Number Catcher game:

www.thenumbercatcher.com/nc/home.php

IT resources in the USA

Dynamo Math is a computer-based intervention program for learners with dyscalculia:

www.dynamomath.com

IT resources in Australia

5-minute maths is a series of videos for parents explaining activities to help your child with maths:

www.speldvic.org.au